Spring

Monarch AND

Milkweed

by Helen Frost
AND
Leonid Gore

Atheneum Books for Young Readers   New York London Toronto Sydney

Acknowledgments

The author thanks Dr. Chip Taylor, of Monarch Watch
at Kansas University, for advice on the text;
Ann Colbert for friendship and knowledge;
and Caitlyn Dlouhy for attentive, joyful editing.
She thanks her parents, Jack and Jean Frost,
for introducing her to Monarch and Milkweed
when she was a small child.

Atheneum Books for Young Readers
An imprint of Simon & Schuster Children's Publishing Division
1230 Avenue of the Americas, New York, New York 10020
Text copyright © 2008 by Helen Frost
Illustrations copyright © 2008 by Leonid Gore
All rights reserved, including the right of reproduction
in whole or in part in any form.
Book design by Ann Bobco
The text for this book is set in Adobe Garamond Pro.
The illustrations for this book are rendered
in acrylic and pastels on paper.
The migration maps on the endpapers were redrawn from
Monarch Watch's website with their permission.
Manufactured in China

2 4 6 8 10 9 7 5 3
Library of Congress Cataloging-in-Publication Data
Frost, Helen, 1949–
Monarch and milkweed / Helen Frost ; illustrated by Leonid Gore.—1st ed.
p.   cm.
ISBN-13: 978-1-4169-0085-6
ISBN-10: 1-4169-0085-3
1. Monarch butterfly—Life cycles—Juvenile literature.
I. Gore, Leonid. II. Title.
QL561.D3F75 2008
595.78'9—dc22
2006034159

Dedicated with love to
Lloyd and Penny, Cameron and Jordan,
beautiful travelers
—H. F.

To the Markman family
—L. G.

In a patch of dirt behind an old red barn,
Milkweed stretches into warm spring air.
Its roots reach deep and wide,
its stem points to the sky.

Monarch spreads her wings and rides the wind—
past white and yellow daisies, across a creek,
heading north.

Milkweed's new leaves push out,
then purple flowers, soft and round and fragrant.

Monarch finds a dandelion,
drinks its nectar and flies on.
She stops again, rests and drinks
and flies again.

Milkweed stretches taller. Two by two,
its leaves spread wide,
sheltering long-legged spiders,
black and orange beetles.

Monarch lights on Milkweed,
drums her feet on Milkweed's flower,
and tastes home.

Milkweed's flowers fall away; green pods push out.
Inside these bumpy fists, new seeds are forming.

Monarch finds a mate
and stays with him all afternoon,
all night, into the morning.
Eggs in her body grow heavy.
    She searches for Milkweed.

A breeze bends Milkweed side to side.
Monarch chooses its best leaf.
Swaying in the breeze with Milkweed,
    she curls her body underneath the leaf
    and glues one pale yellow egg
    to its soft underside.

She flies from milkweed plant to milkweed plant,
stopping on each to lay one shiny egg.

Inside Monarch's egg, a caterpillar forms,
and four days later, pushes out—
shorter than an eyelash,
almost invisible against the leaf's pale green.

It eats the shell that held it,
        then moves across the leaf.
It eats the leaf,
        it grows . . .

and when it grows too big
to fit inside its skin,
it crawls right out,
new skin already formed beneath the old.

Yellow, black, and white, the monarch caterpillar
feeds on Milkweed's bitter leaves
        and grows.

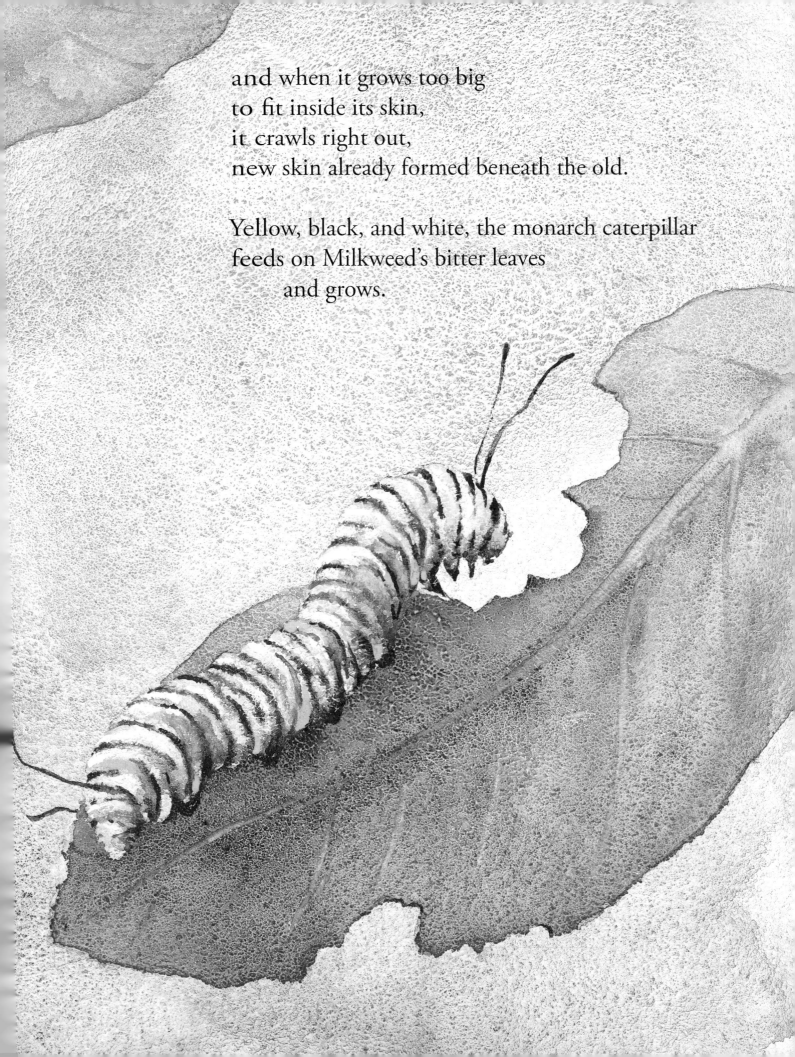

Four times, the caterpillar sheds its skin,
   and then
one evening in late summer,
   it weaves a sturdy pad
under a Milkweed leaf,
   hangs upside down,
      and shapes its body like a J.

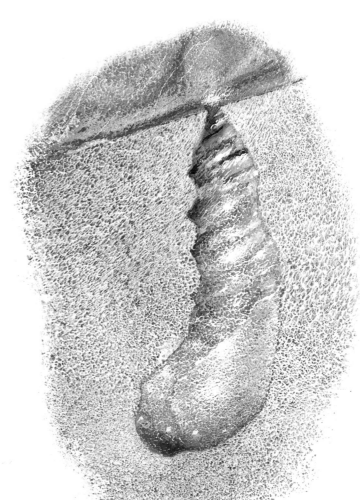

Its feelers droop . . .
   and one last time,
      it sheds its skin—
it twists and turns, and pulls its body up, transforming
into a chrysalis. It hangs beneath the leaf,
a shining jewel,
   jade green, specked with gold.

Twelve days, the monarch chrysalis
      shines in noontime shadows.
Twelve nights,
      it waits under the moon and stars.

It grows darker—gray,
      then black and orange,
      as new monarch wings
      shine through.

Early one morning, the chrysalis splits open—
a new monarch steps out,
    moist wings pressed against her body.
She clings to the clear case of the chrysalis
    as warm air dries her wings.

She opens her wings,
closes them, opens them wide—
a light breeze lifts her,
and she flies.

Milkweed's leaves, now full of holes,
turn yellow,
    then brown.
        Their edges curl, and they begin to fall.

Monarch flies
     from purple zinnia
     to black-eyed Susan,
drinking nectar, getting ready.
     As the days turn cool,
     she turns south toward warmer air
     to begin her longest journey.

Milkweed's pods are full; its seeds are almost ready.
In September's sun, the pods' strong walls turn dry and brown.

Monarch flies and rides the wind,
stopping only long enough
to drink sweet nectar from a field
    of purple asters.
She follows the last flowers of summer
as she flies on
        and on,
        almost two thousand miles—
            all the way to Mexico.

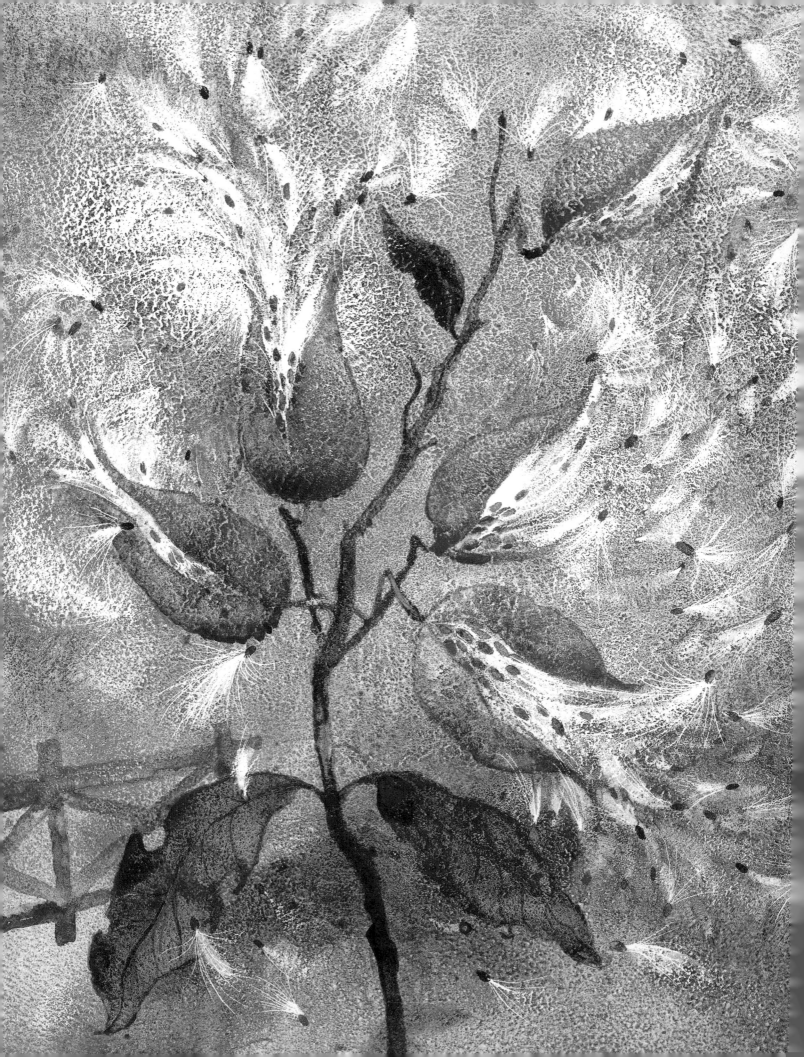

Milkweed's pods split open.
Brown seeds lay close together on a soft, white bed.
October wind catches a silky tendril, opens it,
and lifts a seed into the air,
        carrying it
            out and away,
                across a river,
                    to an old white house.
A kitten reaches up a paw
and bats at the white fluff
        until it disappears.

Rain comes, snow comes, rain comes again.
Sun warms the earth.
Earth warms the seed,
     and under the dirt, it opens.
Roots reach down.
A tip of green presses out and up, toward warmth and light.
Milkweed's first spring leaf unfurls.

Far to the south, in Mexico, Monarch rides the wind toward it.

Author's Note

Each fall, monarch butterflies migrate from eastern North America to Mexico. (Monarchs west of the Rocky Mountains migrate to California). Millions of monarchs gather in Mexico's oyamel fir forests and stay there for the winter. In the spring, monarchs begin the journey back north.

On their northern migration, monarchs mate and lay eggs. Those eggs become caterpillars, then chrysalises. New butterflies emerge and continue the journey. This happens two, three, or four times during the northern migration. The butterflies that complete the return journey are the offspring of those that left in the fall.

The story in this book begins with the final generation on one northern journey and ends with a monarch in the next generation, as that monarch is leaving Mexico to begin the journey north the following spring.

And what about the milkweed?

Each species of butterfly has a host plant—one kind of plant on which the butterfly lays its eggs. When the caterpillars hatch, this is the best kind of plant for them to eat.

Milkweed is the host plant for monarch butterflies. Monarchs can taste with their front feet, and when they land on milkweed, they recognize it as the right place to lay their eggs. Many kinds of milkweed grow in fields along the monarch's journey. When it is time for a monarch to lay her eggs, she looks for milkweed plants.

Each monarch lays hundreds of eggs, usually one egg on each milkweed plant. That way, when the eggs hatch, each caterpillar has enough food. The milkweed leaves have a bitter taste, and monarch caterpillars and butterflies also have that taste, so birds don't like to eat them.

Scientists are trying to learn more about how monarch butterflies find their way to and from the places where they spend the winter. They aren't sure why one butterfly can fly all the way south but it takes several generations to return north. Although we have learned a lot about Monarch and Milkweed, many mysteries remain for future scientists to explore.

For further information, see:
Monarch Watch   http://www.monarchwatch.com
Journey North   http://www.learner.org/jnorth

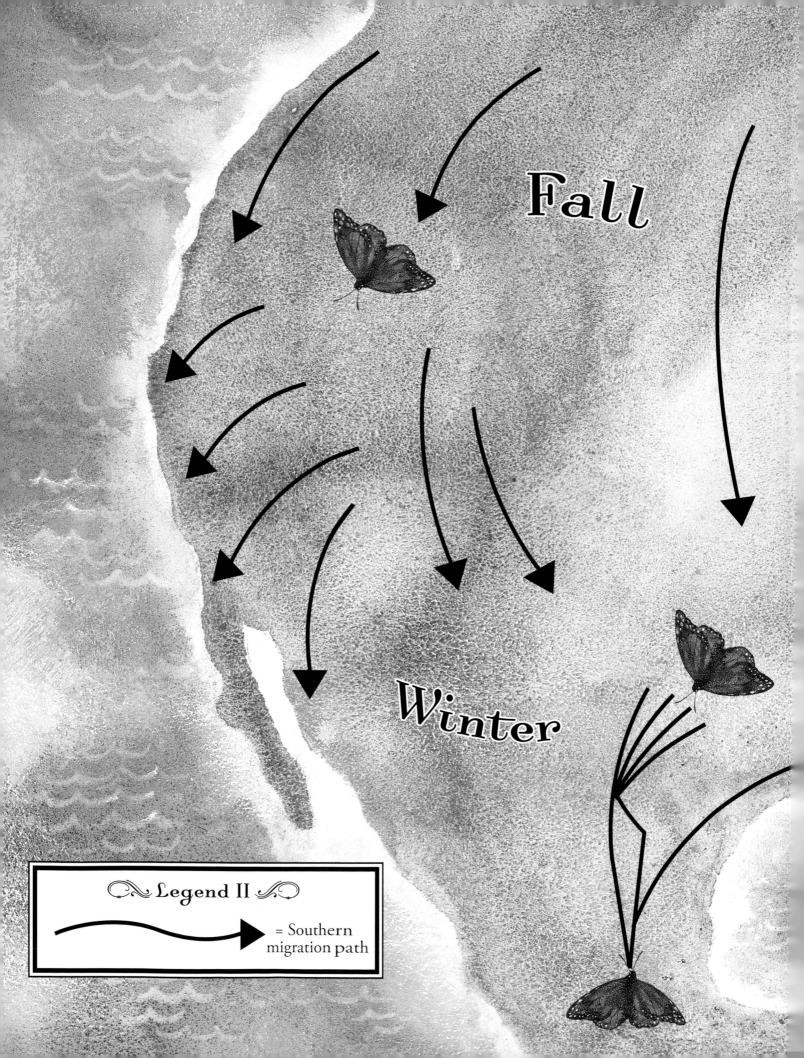